T0065268

UNSHAKABLE
FAITH

FAITH THAT IS ALIVE

Lady E. Nicholas

UNSHAKABLE FAITH
FAITH THAT IS ALIVE

iUniverse books may be ordered through booksellers or by contacting:

iUniverse
1663 Liberty Drive
Bloomington, IN 47403
www.iuniverse.com
844-349-9409

Because of the dynamic nature of the Internet, any web addresses or links contained in this book may have changed since publication and may no longer be valid. The views expressed in this work are solely those of the author and do not necessarily reflect the views of the publisher, and the publisher hereby disclaims any responsibility for them.

Any people depicted in stock imagery provided by Getty Images are models, and such images are being used for illustrative purposes only. Certain stock imagery © Getty Images.

ISBN: 978-1-6632-0142-3 (sc)
ISBN: 978-1-6632-0143-0 (e)

Print information available on the last page.

iUniverse rev. date: 12/17/2020

"A PROPHETIC WORD"

People of God! Hear the word of the LORD. I am sent by
God to herald this message of "UNSHAKABLE FAITH"
into the atmosphere of this world. Your faith must become
ALIVE. You must become unshakable and unmovable in this
Apostolic- prophetic hour we are living in. Without Faith you
cannot please me says the LORD! For this is the hour the world
has been waiting to see. It's *Manifestation Time*. Romans 8:19
says; "For the earnest expectation of the creature waiteth for
the manifestation of the sons of God." Somebody is waiting
for you to go forth in this hour, so, they can receive their
breakthrough. Don't be afraid have faith; "Alive and Unshakable."

DEDICATION

I dedicate this Book to the hundreds of intercessors who
are praying for me. To the Apostolic leaders, Pastors
and Prophetic voices who have declared the word of the
LORD over my life. And to my family "Thank you" for
being patient with me and for supporting me as I seek
to use my gifts to further the Kingdom of God.

CONTENTS

PREFACE

This book is compiled of excerpts from many of the sermons I preached during my seasons of serving the Body of Christ as a local missionary and evangelist. I believe this is the season for this book. It will ignite the faith of new Believers as well as those who have been on the path of salvation for a long time. I guarantee this little book will set your soul on fire and powerfully impact your life. I pray you will sense the love of God and his mighty move, as you read the pages of this book.

Unshakable Faith brings a fresh sense of reality, and the power of Holy Spirit that flows in a believer's life, as we obey the move of the Holy Spirit, especially in the things which are unseen. The Bible says we walk by faith and not by sight. Our faith gives evidence to things that are not seen (Hebrews 11:1). The Bible says in *2nd Kings 6:* that the king of Aram was at war with Israel. Every time he planned to mobilize his forces in a certain place; Elijah the prophet of Israel would send word to the king, and he in turn would send warning to the people, to guard themselves. As time went on, the king of Aram sent his troops to seize the prophet of God.

The Bible says when Elisha's servant awoke one morning he saw the troops, horses and chariots, everywhere. He cried to Elisha, but Elisha commanded him "don't be afraid," in other words have

"FAITH." Elisha assured him, "for there are more on our side than are with them, but the servant could not see into the Unseen world. Fear had gripped his heart. After Elisha prayed for God to open his eyes, he was able to see the horses, and Chariots of fire, God Himself, had surrounding them.

Obeying God in good times as well as the bad times, will add strength to your faith. It will prove that you are a person, capable of working the works of God, An overcomer, who does not waver in your faith. Obeying God will also prove, you are one who have obligated yourself to God, and are born of Him. For whosoever is born of God overcometh the world, and this is the victory that overcometh the world, even our faith (1 John 5:4). For he that doubts is like a wave of the sea, driven and tossed, by the wind (James 1:6b NLT). *"You are an Overcomer."* I release unto you the kind of faith that is alive and unshakable. The kind that will cause you to become UNMOVEABLE!

With pure love
Lady E Nicholas
Laurel Maryland
(2005, 2020)

ACKNOWLEDGEMENT

First giving honor to; My God-Jehovah Saboath (The ONE who
    fights for me)
To Pure Love Ministries original Prayer-chain:
The late Sandra Shell (R.I.P.)
Donna Campbell
Mary Smith
Kathy Queen
Vanessa Shorter
Doris Taylor (Who prayed for my ministry in its conception stages.
    I am eternally grateful)
The late Pastor Andri' Stewart (R.I.P.) And Pastor Maggie Stewart
    (Who encouraged and loved on me when I wanted to quit)
My former Secretary Carolyn Washington (For encouraging me to
    release this work)
Dr. Cedil Booker-Morgan (Who has proven to be a real sister in
    the Lord)
Last but not least; Elder Connie Robinson (Who always believed in
    my ministry & pray for me)

ACKNOWLEDGEMENT

FOREWORD

Pastor Erlene is on a mandate from God to share a word that will cause every believer to move to a place of unshakable faith. When I was introduced to the idea of this book, instantly I realized that because of what the Lord had allowed her to endure it was definitely going to be an experience. While reading through the manuscript on a flight from BWI to RDU Airport to attend a "Will Thou Be Made Whole" Conference, this book was enlightening and empowering, allowing the reader to know that living a life of wholeness begins with a life of *UNSHAKABLE Faith.*

Erlene's scriptural approach and life application intertwined together, brings to life exactly what the outcome is when we mature to a place in God where we totally depend on HIM and no longer lean to our own understanding. She speaks to every level of believer, whether you are a Pastor, Evangelist or Prophet. No matter what gift you possess in the body of Christ, she makes it emphatically clear that unless we live a life of faith, we are living beneath the abundant life that is promised to every believer in God's Word.

I have read many books on different opinions and revelation(s) on faith, but this manuscript takes a direct approach at what unlimited possibilities are available to us when we just believe. Aligning our life and activating our faith even in the face of adversity, even when it seems like God is not going to do it, but because of our *Unshakable Faith* we wait in expectancy until HE performs every word that HE promised.

Unshakable Faith by Erlene Nicholas has caused me to move to another level of faith in my life even while going through what seemingly is a valley experience. I urge you to develop and mature in the Godly principles of faith dealt with in this book and allow your faith to work miraculous wonders in your life. It is then that you too can live a life of *Unshakable Faith*.

May God bless you and keep you in Pure Love and living in divine destiny.

Apostle Pete Mckinnis, Pastor & Founder
Higher Praise Outreach Ministries International
Seat Pleasant, Maryland

CHAPTER 1

TRIALS WILL COME

No one is exempt from trials, tribulations, testing, temptations or personal adversities. Afflictions are a part of everyday life and personal growth. If you and I, who are called children of God, expect to grow from faith to faith and from glory to glory, we must mature to a level of faith that is alive and unshakable.

Romans 8:28 is one of my favorite scriptures, it is a sure word from God. It says: "And we know that all things work together for good to them that love God, to them who are the called according to his purpose."

When we grasp the full meaning of this prophetic word, we can live with peace of mind. In spite of what we see or hear, we will not be moved. When we know that whatever we are going through is working for our good, whether good, bad or indifferent, we will be better able to face the adversities of life, without falling to pieces. When your faith is alive, you can believe God in spite of the tribulations and everyday circumstances, you are **NOT** moved by what you see especially when you are anchored in the Lord.

There is a call of God upon the believer to rise up, therefore, we must arise to the occasion, and believe the word of God for what it's worth. What we go through just because we are saved and sanctified is a reality. The warfare has intensified over the years, and because of the intensity of what we are facing, our minds must be conditioned, so that we are able to face the realities of life and not live our lives in a world of fantasy.

The Bible teaches us in **Hebrews 11:6 (KJV) But without faith it is impossible to please Him: for he that cometh to God must believe that He is and hat He is a rewarder of them that diligently seek Him.**

Many people today operate in lack of faith and fear. There are Christian Leaders who are appointed to lead the people of God, yet they are afraid to exercise belief in the Word of God for their lives as well as for their ministries.

The reason for our lack of faith is **disbelief** and **unbelief. Disbelief** is the result of the lack of faith in the Word of God. When a person lacks in their faith, they are without faith, their faith is missing or their faith is deficient. This type of faith lacks the nutriment it needs to promote the proper development of one's spiritual faith in God. When we operate in disbelief, and things are not going the way we plan, we begin to worry and complain. We try to convince ourselves that God has forgotten about us and we become plagued with a mind to give up or just simply throw in the towel.

Unbelief denotes absence of positive belief or a refusal to believe. The person that operates in unbelief has faith, but not positive faith, this person refuses to believe that God can come any other way, but the way he or she want God to come. Remember, we serve a Sovereign Lord, He can do whatever He wants to do, when or where He wants to, and how and in whom He wants to do it. A person who exercises unbelief is partial when it comes to believing God, this type of faith will cause one to miss the move of God, because there is a lack of confidence in the Word of God and genuine people of God.

When one operates in this type of spirit, he or she may miss both the message and the messenger.

I have never seen in all of my years of serving the Lord so many people, especially church leaders, who have no guts to believe that God is NOT a man that He should lie and that God is still in control, in spite of all the chaos and confusion in the world. Let me clarify that when I say church leaders, I am not necessarily speaking about pastors only. There are Auxiliary Leaders, Youth Leaders/Pastors, Missionaries, Elders, Deacons, Sunday School and Bible Teachers. These are those we depend on and look up to as role models.

If you fall in any of these categories anywhere in the church, you are a leader and I am speaking to you as well. They quote Scriptures, attend revival after revival and yet some still have so little of what it takes to please the Lord. All I'm saying is, it's time for us to go beyond the norm, of just singing, shouting, speaking in tongues, falling out and having church per usual. There is so much more. God wants us to be complete in Him, and that does not mean that all will be well, all the time. It does mean that when the worst thing that can happen to you does happen, you are still able to stand on the promises of God. We must believe that God's Word is the truth that will set us free. It is bound to bring true deliverance and validate assurance deep down on the inside, of the fact that all things do work together for good to them that love God, and are the called according to His purpose. When you understand the call of God on your life, there is an inner urging to fulfill destiny and a deep hunger to please the Father.

Hebrews 11:6 (KJV) says: But without faith it is impossible to please Him: for he that cometh to God must believe that he is, and that he is a rewarder of them that diligently seek him.

As ministers of the Gospel of Jesus Christ, we have an awesome responsibility to not only set ourselves in position to be a blessing to our Fathers in the Gospel, but also to be an example to those we lead, in light of this, we need to know that our first responsibility is to please God and obey his commands.

3

So if you ignore the least commandment and teach others to do the same, you will be called the least in the Kingdom of Heaven. But anyone who obeys God's laws and teaches them will be called great in the Kingdom of Heaven. But I warn you—unless your righteousness is better than the righteousness of the teachers of religious law and the Pharisees, you will never enter the Kingdom of Heaven! (Matthew 5:19-20 NLT)

God always required more from us, than we are willing to give. In this era of Christendom, people want to be great, but the Bible says, if you want to be great, you must obey the laws of God, better than the one who teaches you and in return you must teach others to obey them also. Our gift is to bring God glory, it is not for self-gain. **Our motives must be pure.**

We live in a society where people expect to get where they are going overnight, some call it a microwave society, where people expect to be overnight wonders. I have come to realize that there is no short cut in the process God takes us through. To get us to where God wants you to be, **YOU WILL GO THROUGH.** Sometimes you may have to pass through the waters, and through the rivers, you may even have to walk through the fire. (Isaiah 43:2) But He promised, "I will be with thee."

DO NOT BE MOVED

Hebrews 3:1-2 (KJV) says: Wherefore, holy brethren partakers of the heavenly calling, consider the Apostle and High Priest of our profession, Christ Jesus; Who was faithful to him that appointed him, as also Moses was faithful in all his house.

This is the reason why our faith must be unshakable, for if we are wavering in our faith, we are not pleasing God. God does not want us to be moved by what we are going through, as unreal as this may seem, you may wake up one Monday morning and find out that your car has been repossessed, on Tuesday your lights get turned off, Wednesday, the gas gets turned off, on Thursday you have no monies for transportation to and from work. But the Lord makes a way. Friday comes your husband gets paid but decided to leave. Or he spends his entire paycheck on drugs, gambling, or just life on the fast tracks. The telephone bill is still due, there is no food for the children to eat, one of your sons is on drugs, your daughter runs away, your baby has some type of virus. Mentally, emotionally, physically, financially and spiritually you are in a rut.

The Lord does not allow you to tell your prayer partner, or your pastor- if you have one or your best friend, because he is going to get the glory out of your life and the credit due to Him for deliverance you thought was impossible. My point is, God does not want us to be shaken by the circumstances that challenges us in our everyday life. He wants us to **believe that he is, and that he is a rewarder of them that diligently seek him.**

Somehow you are able to gather up enough strength to come to God in prayer. In spite of what you are going through right now, there is a ray of hope, that brighter days are ahead, for his anger endureth but a moment; in his favor is life; weeping may endure for a night, joy cometh in the morning (Psalms 30:5). God is a rewarder of them that diligently seek him; those that are called seek after God, not after prosperity, not after prophecy, or after personal gain, but **after God.**

But seek ye first the Kingdom of God, and His righteousness; and all these things shall be added unto you. (Matthew 6:33 KJV)

In Hebrews 3:1-2, the Apostle Paul exhorts the believer to keep Jesus in the forefront of our minds. Notice he called us holy brethren, partakers of the heavenly calling. We are not only brethren, but brethren of Christ, holy, not only in profession, but also in what we practice in our hearts and in our lives, partakers of the Spirit of grace that comes from Heaven. You do not have to be moved by hard trials and tribulations. The process of God is painful at times, but know that there is purpose in your pain. Have faith in God, he is able to see you through. Faith is a spiritual force, it is God's creative power. God is always working to make us better Christians,

Ministers and Witnesses of the Gospel of Jesus Christ. Remember Jesus is our High Priest. Paul reminds us to consider him as the Apostle of our profession, the great revealer of the faith we profess to hold, the hope which we profess to have and the intercession which we profess to depend upon, for the forgiveness of our sins and acceptance with God.

Hebrews 4:14-16 (KJV) says: Seeing then that we have a great High Priest, that is passed into the heavens, Jesus the Son of God, let us hold fast our profession. For we have not an high priest, which cannot be touched with the feeling of our infirmities; but was in all points tempted like as we are, yet without sin. Let us therefore come boldly unto the throne of grace, that we may obtain mercy and find grace to help in time of need.

As much as we dislike being confronted by trials, tribulations and personal adversities, we must endure the soundness of this doctrine.

Psalm 34:19 (KJV) says: Many are the afflictions of the righteous: but the Lord delivereth him out of them all.

Trials will come, but God's divine promises enables us to go through and experience the awesomeness of His care and the sufficiency of His grace. Jesus said unto me, my grace is sufficient for thee: for my strength is made perfect in weakness. My brothers and sisters in the Lord, as you go through the trials of this life, because they will come, let the Apostle Paul's testimony enlighten you and testify to the glory of God.

Paul declared in **II Cor. 12:9b (KJV): Most gladly therefore will I rather glory in my infirmities, that the power of Christ may rest upon me.**

Remember, there is no short cut to complete the process for what God has ordained for us to be. So then, make up your mind, I would rather have the power of Christ rest upon me.

DELIVERANCE WILL COME

Your faith must motivate action. Faith is not what you say; it is what you do, with what God has spoken. Faith is taking the word of God for what it is worth. When you take God at His Word, you are able to stand on it, walk in it, act upon it, without first seeing it come to pass. Faith is taking God at His Word, because he is a trustworthy God. I find no fault in Him, no fallacy in the written Word of God. He has been to me exactly who He says He Is.

God wants to impart to his children the kind of faith that can conquer anything. Faith that will change our life's attitude towards Him. When you believe that God is trustworthy, everything you do, say or think is shaped by your conviction. This enables you to respond to God wholeheartedly.

Your faith is now alive and unshakable. So even though you do not see the promise of God materializing as yet, you have this certainty that God will deliver and that He is not only who He says He is, but He is also able. Faith is the confident assurance that my deliverance is going to happen, it is waiting for me up ahead, even though I cannot see it naturally. I should be able to visualize it.

Hebrew 11:1 (KJV) says: Now faith is the substance of things hoped for the evidence of things not seen.

The best of us think too little of Christ or too slightly of Him at times. I walked into the ladies room at work one day and there were two ladies on their way out, one white and one black. Please note this is not a racial issue, I am only using this incident as an example to show the mindset or the way we think at times.

The white lady said to the black lady, "I spent nine hours balancing my checkbook yesterday." The black lady replied with amazement, and a high pitched voice, "nine hours, you must have a lot of money, it only takes me five minutes to balance mine." I don't know why, this seemed so funny to me at the time, but it was the most hysterical thing that I had ever heard. I was in that ladies room laughing so hard the tears rolled down my cheeks. All of a sudden the Holy Spirit spoke, *"Oh so you think that's funny? With man it is impossible but with God all things are possible, all it takes is faith."*

Here I was thinking she is crazy to even think that lady has that much money, it would take her nine hours to balance her checkbook. After all, if she has that much money, why is she working? If I had that much money, my accountant would be balancing my checkbook, it certainly would not have been me.

I did not even consider the fact that God is great and He is able to do exceeding abundantly above all that we can ask or think, the Word was so far from my mind concerning what I had just heard, I simply doubted what I heard was even possible at the time I heard it, especially since the woman was at work. That was my justification. That is certainly not where I would have been, if I had that much money in my bank account and had to use nine hours to balance it, even if I was President of the World Bank. But God's Word does not lie.

Ephesians 3:20 (KJV) says: *Now unto him who is able to do exceeding abundantly above all that we ask or think according to the power that worketh in us.* The Greek word for "exceeding abundantly" is **Perissos:** meaning *Superabundantly.* God wants to do above and beyond our imagination. Our finite mind's cannot even imagine, what God has prepared for us because what He wants to do has not yet been invented, it has not yet been materialized, but it is certainly possible, therefore we need foresight, insight and revelation to even fathom the extraordinary things, God wants to do in our lives. People of God get ready for that which is above the greatest abundance. Something good is about to happen in your life. You are going to be amazed, beyond measure and wonder.

I encourage you to hold fast to your profession, look unto Jesus the Author and Finisher of your faith. He is your Redeemer, the Messiah, your Healer, your Savior, your Deliverer and Friend.

Whatever he promised you, charge it to his account, he has already paid the price. Jesus already picked up your tab, just remember there is nothing impossible with God. Paul encouraged us in Hebrews 3 to be steadfast, and to persevere to the end as Christ who was faithful to him that appointed him, therefore Christ is more, worthy of glory, than Moses. Moses was only a faithful servant, but Jesus Christ, the eternal Son of God, is the rightful owner and sovereign ruler of the Church. Whose house we are, if we hold fast the confidence and the rejoicing of the hope, firmly to the end.

Faith gives us the power we need to be overcomers in this life. The desire of every Christian is to stand before the Father and hear—*Well done, thy good and faithful servant*, but this will never be unless we get rid of fear.

Revelation 21:8 (KJV) says: But the fearful, and unbelieving, and the abominable, and murderers, and whoremongers, and sorcerers, and idolaters, and all liars, shall have their part in the lake which burneth with fire and brimstone: which is the second death.

Fear is a killer, while Faith is a life giver.

DO YOU BELIEVE

Abraham was considered righteous by God because of his faith. It is possible to be in right standing with God in one area of your life, yet lack the courage you need to believe that He is able to work miracles in another area of your life. Abraham's life proved to us that even those of great faith may sometimes have doubts.

God made a covenant between Him and Abraham. It was established as a covenant of promise. It was an assurance of God's kindness and good-will towards Abraham and his seed in many generations to come.

Genesis17:7 (KJV) says: And I (God) will establish my covenant between me and thee and thy seed after thee in their generations for an everlasting covenant, to be a God unto thee, and to thy seed after thee.

God in this passage of scripture displayed his role as a Father who left to his son (Abraham) an inheritance, and not only to his son, but he also left enough for his grandchildren (Isaac), his great grandchildren (Jacob) and his great-great grandchildren (Joseph generation). In all that God had promised Abraham, he came to a point in his life where he was unsure of the promises God had made to him. Abraham wavered in his faith.

CHAPTER 2

AN EVERLASTING COVENANT

God's promise to Abraham dealt with his faith. The covenant with Abraham shows that faith is the only way to be saved.

Genesis 17:7-10 (KJV) says: And I will establish my covenant between me and thee and thy seed after thee in their generations for an everlasting covenant, to be a God unto thee, and to thy seed after thee. And I will give unto thee and to thy seed after thee, the land wherein thou art a stranger, all the land of Canaan, for an everlasting possession; and I will be their God. And God said unto Abraham, thou shalt keep my covenant therefore, thou, and thy seed after thee in their generations. This is my covenant, which ye shall keep, between me and you and thy seed after thee; Every man child among you shall be circumcised.

God visited Abram 13 years after the birth of his son Ishmael, (not the promised child), He made Abram a promise that he would be the father of many nations. Isaac (the promised child) was not born until approximately 25 years later. Could you imagine, waiting 25 years for your promise to come to pass. You must have faith and patience. Notice, after God changed Abram's name and told him that he would be God to him and his seed and would give them the land of Canaan; (the Promised Land). The Bible says that God appeared to Abram in all his glory and Abram fell on his face while God spoke to him.

Abram was a very humble man, so when God appeared to Abram in his Shekinah glory, Abram humbled himself by falling on his face before God. Abram by faith humbled himself because he realized he was in God's glorious presence and that he was unworthy. How would you have responded? If you experienced the brightness of God's glorious presence, would you fall on your face and humble yourself before God or would you become arrogant and filled with pride. I believe one of the lessons here is that, we should guard ourselves against arrogance when the Lord begins to reveal himself to us and bless us in very special ways. After all Abram was a rich man, because God had made him rich. (Genesis 13:2) Yet, he was still in waiting for the "Promised Child." And he remained humble as he waited upon the Lord.

DO NOT BE DESTROYED

Fear is the opposite of faith. It is Satan's destructive power, the substance of things not desirable to the believer. Faith is the means of things hoped for, the evidence or proof of things not seen with the natural eye, but are eternal. You must be able to see beyond your present circumstances into the spiritual realm in order that you might tap into the type of faith that **is alive and unshakable.** If faith is belief without evidence and we believe that God is faithful, then we should have the kind of confidence that it takes to believe in a Trustworthy God no matter what comes our way. However, this is not the case in the life of many Christians. Fear of the unknown often brings an uneasiness of not being in control of their own lives. My friends, fear will destroy you; it will rob you of your peace of mind. I remember a time in my life when I was so afraid. I was afraid to believe God, afraid to step out in faith and do the will of the Father for my life, afraid of what people would think, afraid that

I would fail, afraid I wasn't good enough; until one day I realized that I needed deliverance. This was not a reverence or awe of the presence of God, this was a doubtful or timid type of fear: And now I can stand in the face of opposition. And not be moved, because not only does God have my back, I have faith to believe that *GOD CAN.*

2 Timothy 1:7 (KJV): For God has not given us a spirit of fear; but of power, and of love, and of a sound mind.

When you are going through and you are unsure of the promises of God in your life, it is time to **worship.** Worship imparts power into your spirit. Abraham was going through because he desperately wanted a child and at one point he thought he was never likely to have any children of his own. Abraham went through a season of depression and he complained to God. In the midst of his complaint he prayed and worshiped and God strengthened and confirmed his faith and Abraham believed God again. God preached to Abraham himself from the sermon title. **"I am the Lord Jehovah."** God assured Abraham in this message to him that He (God) **was El Shaddai, God Almighty, The All-Sufficient One.** God spoke a Word to Abraham to encourage and strengthen him. Are you in a season of depression right now? Is there something in your life that you are complaining to God about?

Your life, your ministry, your Church, your job, your health, your finances, your children, your wife or your husband. Stop yourself; believe God, and know that you are blessed. He is Jehovah. There is a word from the Lord to encourage and strengthen you; But my God *shall supply all your need according to his riches in glory by Christ Jesus* (Philippians 4:19 KJV). The fact is do you believe it?

WE ARE BLESSED

We are a blessed people and we have a right to the promises of God's Kingdom. We have been blessed from the foundations of this world, even before you and I entered into our Mother's womb we were blessed. Christians have an assurance that God will do for us what we ask of him through faith, according to his will for our lives. How do we know the will of God for our life? We know the will of God for our lives through His word. God's Will is His Word and His Word is His Will. We understand the Will of God for our lives, when we understand His Word and we understand His Word through faith.

Romans 10:17 (KJV) says: So then faith cometh by hearing, and hearing by the word of God.

Our Christian life is based on "faith." You and I will never be able to please God without it, so how can you say honestly that you have faith, when you have not set yourself in position to hear God's word. Some of you who are reading this book right now, have not been to Bible Study in years. You won't have a problem going for a night cap at some Bar and Restaurant after getting off late from work on any given night, but your excuse for not going to Bible Study is that you work late. You may even consider what I'm saying as judgmental, but really, have you considered how important God is to you, because the truth is you cannot serve God and mammon. Stop being afraid to stand up for what is right.

The reason why some of us still do not know the will of God for our lives is because what we are hearing is not sound doctrine and because some of us do not know what God's word says about what we hear. We believe everything we hear without discerning the spirit in which the Word was given.

John 15:7 (KJV) says: If ye abide in me, and my words abide in you, ye shall ask what ye will, and it shall be done unto you.

When you allow God's word to abide in you, his will also abides in you. So many times Christians expect the word of God to abide in them and work for them, yet they have not searched the scriptures, meditated on them, and allowed the word to motivate their human spirit. Prayer and fasting activates the anointing in our lives. It brings a certain level of sensitivity in the spirit. The Bible says that some things only come by prayer and fasting. Most Christians want to be blessed, but do not want to live their lives in submission to God.

You are already blessed, just to be a Christian, but there are deeper depths and higher heights in God and it is yours to attain. Let the word of God dwell in your inner most being and ask God what you will. Remember if it takes twenty-five years to come to past, wait for the manifestation; God cannot and He will not lie.

Work While You Wait

It is a blessing to be in Covenant relationship with the Lord. So many people today have religion, but have no idea what it's like to experience true intimacy with the Lord. They can talk a good game, but the walk does not line up with the talk.

Romans 10:1-3 (AMP) says: Brothers and sisters, my heart's desire and my prayer to God for Israel is for their salvation. For I testify about them that they have a certain enthusiasm for God, but not in accordance with [correct and vital] knowledge [about Him and His purposes]. For not knowing about God's righteousness [which is based on faith], and seeking to establish their own [righteousness based on works], they did not submit to God's righteousness.

We want our relationship with God to be according to clear biblical perspectives, not because we seek to establish a means of salvation on our own. Some people think because they do good deeds, that makes them good persons, and so they have a right to heaven. My dear friends, the Word of God says in John 3:3: unless you are born again, you can never see the kingdom of God. We are truly a blessed people and our covenant relationship with God must be according to the vital and correct knowledge we have of Him as our Master.

Waiting on the promises of God to materialize at times will cause uneasiness. If we are not careful, like Abraham and Sarah we may seek for other means by which to bring about God's promises in our lives. While you wait on the Lord, work out your soul's salvation. Working to upbuild the Kingdom of God can keep your mind stayed on the Lord. It can also keep you out of trouble while you wait for God's timing. Unfortunately, one of the things we have not yet grasp in the Body of Christ, is concerning the timing of God and His promises. God's timing is far more important than His promise. And when we try to speed up the process, to bring to pass the promise, we miss God.

There are many today who finds themselves out of the perfect will of God and have settled for his permissive will, because they were not patient enough to wait on the Lord. You may get what you want but is it in God's timing. Abraham and Sarah got Ishmael, but he was not what God had promised, and he ended up causing them pain. You may think that you are stepping out by faith, although God had already spoken. But instead you stepped out for fear that your family and friends would no longer approve of you. I encourage you today, if you are out of God's perfect will it's time to get back in the boat. There is joy to be found in what pleases God the most, I would often share with my church family, obedience to God brings peace, while disobedience brings disaster. What God permit you to do only sustains you for a moment, and when that moment passes you by, even that thing you desired so badly will not satisfy your soul. Some people will bite their noses off, and spite their own face trying to have their own way.

Have you ever been in a situation where someone deliberately tried to stop you? Don't get mad, just keep on working while you wait on the Lord. While the haters, like the young folks of our day call them, try to hate on you and rob you of your joy keep waiting on the Lord and see what happens. For the Lord promise, those who bless you shall prosper and those who curse or try to hurt you shall be cursed or cut off. There is no place like the perfect will of God. And in the perfect will of God we are to exercise patience. The kind of patience that makes the Joy of the Lord our strength, while we wait.

Let us pray: *Heavenly Father, we come to you asking that you give us the courage we need to wait on you. We thank you that all things do work together for our good, Father, grant us peace and teach us how to wait on your timing; give us strength to work while it is day for your word says the night comes when no man will be able to work, keep us in your perfect and divine will in Jesus Name. Father we thank you that as we wait upon the Lord and remain in good courage, you will powerfully anoint us to impact every nation, while we continually endure all trials and tribulations in the Name of Jesus Christ we pray. Amen!*

CHAPTER 3

OBEYING GOD

God kept his promise to Abraham, he has not revoked it. He saved Abraham through faith and blessed the world through Abraham by sending Jesus as one of his descendants. (Matthew 1) Circumstances may change, but God remains the same. He is a constant God, he is the same yesterday, today and forever, he never breaks his promises. Obedience in our lives brings us into mutual agreement with the spirit of God, through the Holy Spirit. As you and I obey the Word of God we begin to understand Him. God made a contract between himself and Abraham with terms that were very simple. Abraham was to believe in God and obey him. God, in return, will give unto Abraham's heir wealth and power. Most contracts that are made between two or more parties are even trade of equal value. You give something and in return receive something in equal value. When we covenant with God, his blessings far outweigh whatever we must give up.

I Corinthians 2:9-12 (KJV): But as it is written, Eye hath not seen, nor ear heard, neither have entered into the heart of man, the things which God hath prepared for them that love him. But God hath revealed them unto us by his Spirit: for the Spirit searcheth all things, yea, the deep things of God. For what man knoweth the things of man, save the spirit of man which is in him? even so the things of God knoweth no man, but the Spirit of God. Now we have received, not the spirit of the world, but the spirit which is of God; that we might know the things that are freely given to us of God.

It is by the light, the revelation of obedience to God, having the mind of Christ and his Word richly dwelling in us, which enable us to understand revealed truth. God has to reveal them to us by his spirit. Notice, what the Apostle writes: Eye hath not seen, nor ear heard, neither entered into the heart of man; in other words, the greatest truths of the gospel are in things which are not in the realm of humanity. They are spirit and life. We cannot tap into them by our own natural ability, again, God has to reveal them to us by His Spirit.

If this was the real world to the human spirit, we would have no need for the light of God's revelation. When we accept the Lord Jesus Christ into our hearts as Lord and Savior our human spirit becomes alive and regenerated by the word of truth. The truth will then make you free, free to believe, thus having faith in the true and living God. Before the rebirth of your human spirit you were bound by sin and shame, but now you are free and liberated by God's Spirit. Your soul is at rest, at peace, restored to obey the word of God and to be a blessing. If you are still bound by sin and shame, you may be selfish and probably not free at all with your giving. Giving is a token of your obedience.

Token of Obedience

The Apostle Paul wrote: Eye hath not seen, nor ear heard, neither had it entered into the heart of man, the things which God hath prepared for **those that love Him**. Waiting on God is a token of our love for him. I remember when I first received the call of God upon my life. I waited on Him before I made any moves, because

I was afraid of messing up. I made sure before I make any moves, I really heard from God. I had this notion though, that God needed to wait on me to make up my mind to accept the call. The Word says: There are things that God hath prepared for those that love and wait for him; but we must obey while we wait. Those with servant hearts wait upon the LORD. However, we need to understand we're **not** doing God a favor. God wants our obedience. In the midst of my struggles to obey God, I realized accepting the call of God brought peace into my life. In the midst of everyday circumstances, disappointments and failures, I can still have peace if I'm obedient to God. God was not moved, He was not struggling, He was still on the throne. His schedule had not been interrupted, He is still in control and right state of mind. I was struggling, losing sleep, could not think straight because of my failure to be obedient and to accept the call of God upon my life. Thank God for sovereign deliverance.

This all resulted because disobedience to God brings **misery.** Some Christians face a similar type of struggle, except they are unable to wait on God to move in their lives the way He desires. They struggled because they assumed God is not moving fast enough; so, they accept the role of helping God out. Abraham and Sarah received a promise from God concerning the thing He hath prepared for them. Their heir was to be a child born from their own womb. Now, in our day and culture we would consider what Abraham and Sarah did as adulterous, but notice Sarah gave her consent. Sarah was desperate for this promise to come to pass, and so she acted according to a law during her day that said if a wife was unable to bear children, she could give her slave girl to her husband as a wife for the sake of bearing children. Notice this same practice in Genesis 29 and 30. Both of Jacob's wives: Leah and Rachel were in competition to see who can give Jacob the most children. During those periods when either of them thought they would have no more children, they both gave their servants; Zilpah Leah's servant and Bilhah Rachel's servant to their husband Jacob, for the sake of having more children.

There was also a law back in those days that if a man did not have an heir, he may adopt one of his slaves as his heir. That is why when God promised Abraham in a vision He would protect him and his reward will be great, Abraham's response to God was "what good is all your blessings when I don't even have a son, my servant Eliezer of Damascus will inherit all my wealth" (Genesis 15). God assured Abraham he will have a son. However, Sarah failed to realize God had everything prepared for them already; all they would have to do is wait on Him. She did not rely on the discerner, so instead she used desperate measures to get the desired result. We must be careful not to run ahead of God. We will cause ourselves much misery when we do. We must have faith that God is able to see us through any and every situation in our lives. In all that Abraham and Sarah went through they received the promise, but only in God's timing. If you really love the Lord, I encourage you to wait on Him, be of good courage and obey him faithfully, because He is not a man that he should lie. Whatever He promised, He is able to bring it to pass.

Isaiah 64:4 (KJV) says: For since the beginning of the world men have not heard, not perceived by the ear, neither hath the eye seen, O God, beside thee, what he hath prepared for him that waiteth for him.

OBEDIENCE TO THE TRUTH

Obedience is faith and faith is the initial act of obedience in the new life. If you are a born again believer reading this book you have a new life now, old things are passed away all things have become new. When we hear the Word of God we respond by faith. Faith comes by hearing the word of God, which is the truth. When you obey God you give the only possible evidence that in your heart, you believe God. Something doesn't become true just because you believe in it, you must act in faith. When we are fully persuaded of the truth of God's word, the result is faith.

Disobedience is the evidence of unbelief or disbelief: remember unbelief is the result of a refusal to believe the truth. Disbelief is a result of lacking nourishing faith. Deficient faith stops proper spiritual maturity. So make sure what you believe is of God. Take note that God's will is his word and you must search the scriptures if you are to know what God's word says. You cannot obey the truth, if you don't know the truth and you cannot know the truth if you don't read or listen to the word.

So often people use the excuse that they don't understand the Bible, so they don't read the Bible, and they come to Church expecting the Person's in five-fold ministry to expound on the word for them; which is ok, but applying the Word of God to your own lives and reading your bibles however, are your responsibility. The Word of God is light. There is nothing wrong with expecting the Word to be broken down to you by those in the five-fold ministry, what would be wrong of you however is not knowing if the word you are hearing is truly the word of God. It is your responsibility to read and apply the word to your own lives, if you hear it right, and apply it right, you can also live it right.

We should always check the content of what is written or spoken so that we would not be fooled by false prophets on the rise. God did not ask us to study to be approved by man, but unto Him and if we work hard at studying, we will not be ashamed, but we will be able to rightly divide the word of truth. When you know how to rightly divide the word of truth, when you hear the word, something will happen in your spirit because faith cometh by hearing, so, also, when you hear something that is contrary to the word of truth. A red flag will go up in your spirit.

It's time now to study, listen and know the voice of God. Acts 17:10-12: ...And the brethren immediately sent away Paul and Silas by night unto Berea: who coming thither went into the synagogue of the Jews. These were more noble than those in Thessalonica, in that they received the word with all readiness of mind, and searched the scriptures daily, whether those things

were so. Therefore many of them believed; also of honourable women which were Greeks, and of men, not a few.

The people in Berea opened the scriptures for themselves and searched for Truths to verify or disprove the message they heard. You should always compare what you hear and read with what the Bible says. Any person who preaches and teaches the infallible, uncompromised, unadulterated word of God will attempt to avoid contradicting God's true message. We believe, because we are persuaded that what we believe is true; so then what is truth? Is it just what we want to believe or is it what the Word of God says, even if we do not want to believe it? If I don't believe God is whom He says He is, it does not mean that He is not God.

God made an oath with Abraham to confirm his promises. In other words, God bound Himself with an oath as an affirmation. Affirmations are good for you as long as they are put in proper perspective. God's word will not work effectively in our lives when we are operating outside of His will and purpose for our lives, no matter how much we affirm or receive confirmation. Obedience is better than sacrifice. Be careful of the oaths that you make. People have bound themselves with an oath. His covenant with Abraham includes "I will bless them that bless thee and curse him that curseth thee."

Acts 23:21:...But do not thou yield unto them: for there lie in wait for him of them more than forty men, which have bound themselves with an oath, that they will neither eat nor drink till they have killed him: and now are they ready, looking for a promise from thee.

The Bible says that certain Jews more than forty of them conspired together to kill Paul. Their desire to kill him was so strong that they formed themselves under a formal ecclesiastical curse to excommunicate Paul, indicating to invoke the worse kind of calamity upon themselves, if they did not kill him. To incline to do evil and intend to do it is a direct contempt against God's providence. What they were doing was directly against the order of

God's word; anyone who would be bold enough to ask to be cursed if they do not do so and so, or if so and so doesn't happen, based upon what they have spoken, is speaking the language of hell and asking for trouble. I remember being part of a ministry and under a pastor who would back up what he would prophesy, by saying "if God did not show me or tell me what I just said may God curse me and my family" that is foolish. We all are human and have at one point or another miss God. As men and women of God we must know that we are anointed to be who God has called us to be. All we need to do is speak God's Word if God said it, it will come to pass.

We contaminate God's Word, when we look to man for validation. Death and life are in the power of your tongue, be sure when you speak the Word for God that you do not speak curses but speak life. Remember disobedience does bring curses into someone's life. God does not want His people to be cursed, but to be blessed. That is why He warns us about disobedience (Deuteronomy 28).

These Jews believed in themselves that they were able to bring this wicked device to pass, against Paul. They came to the Chief Priests and Elders and said "We have bound ourselves under a great curse that we will eat nothing until we have slain Paul." They also wanted the Chief Priest and Elders to ask the Chief Captain to bring Paul down to the council the next day under a false pretense so that they can kill him on the way. (Acts 23: 14-15). Cursed is the man that trusteth in man and blessed is the man that trusteth in the Lord.

Blessed is the man that walketh not in the counsel of the ungodly, nor standeth in the way of sinners...(Psalms 1:1 (KJV)). Remember, God is in control.

CHAPTER 4

SEASONS OF CONFRONTATION

Has God ever placed you in a position, where it seemed like you just appeared on the scene? In some cases it appeared as though you had just dropped out of sight? Well, Elijah the Prophet who was of the inhabitants of Gilead, whose name means "My God Jehovah is He," was one of the first in the long line of important Prophets, whom God sent to both Israel and Judah. Elijah appeared on the scene during a time when Israel, the Northern Kingdom had no faithful Kings throughout its history. Ahab, who was Israel's present King, was leading the people in worshiping Baal, who was a heathen god.

During this time there were a few Priests left from the tribe of Levi, but most of them had gone to Judah. The Priest appointed by Israel's Kings were corrupt or ineffective and here comes Elijah to interrupt the normal flow of things in the Northern Kingdom. Ahab certainly did not appreciate Elijah's arrival because he was use to being the king who sinned boldly. Anytime you find yourself in a place so plagued with a bad leader, start seeking God for direction.

The Bible makes it clear that Elijah appeared somewhat abruptly. He drops so to speak out of the clouds as if he was without a father, a mother and without descent. This made some of the Jews think that Elijah was an angel sent from Heaven. Paul assures us however, that he was a man subject to like passions just like we are. Elijah knew what his purpose for being in Israel was, so he wasted no time in confronting King Ahab. He proclaimed to the King in whose power it was to reform the land and prevent the judgement of God, that unless he repented and reformed the land, judgement will be brought upon his land.

SPIRITUALLY CORRUPTED

We live in a day and time when people go to the church, they carry their Bibles, give their tithes and offerings, they even boast about what they do in the church and for the church, all as an act of religiosity, some of them do not have a real relationship with God the Father. Some do not read their bibles regularly, some never have time for devotion and concentrated prayer, some do not have real fellowship with the Holy Spirit and some only come crying to Jesus when they are in trouble. They have no idea what true worship is all about and they have religion but no real relationship. These are the ones who are like roaring lions (1 Peter 5:8), they will devour you if they can, they are usually selfish, cannot stand to see another person progress in God, they are normally jealous of others but they profess to know Christ. These are the hell-raisers in our churches. They are spiritually corrupted.

God is taking his people from religion to relationship, from tradition to truth, from ritual to right standing, from hopelessness to hope, from carnality to spirituality, from faith to faith and from glory to glory. God is looking for a people who are totally sold out to Him no matter what comes their way. I heard someone say, "Come hell or high water, I won't turn back." Esther puts it like this "If I perish let me perish I am going to see the King." The children of Israel during this time needed deliverance and God knew it. God knows when you and I need deliverance. Some of us only need deliverance from self. Self is usually the reason for most Christian's spiritual corruption.

With no King or Priests to bring God's word to the people, God raised up Prophets like Elijah to rescue Israel from its moral and spiritual decline. For the next 300 years these men and women were to be instrumental in both, Israel and Judah, encouraging the *people and leaders* to turn back to God. I believe that God is raising up true Prophets, men and women of God who would boldly stand for righteousness. Men and women, so open to the power of God that when they speak and pray earnestly, God will in return confirm the counsel of his servants. How do we know a true Prophet? That which he speaks will come to pass.

I Kings 17:1 (KJV): And Elijah the Tishbite, who was of the inhabitants of Gilead, said unto Ahab, As the Lord God of Israel liveth, before whom I stand, there shall not be dew nor rain these years, but according to my word.

King Ahab was spiritually corrupted. The Bible makes it clear that he exceeded all his predecessors in wickedness. The Bible says, he did more to provoke God to anger than any of the Kings of Israel that had gone before him.

I Kings 16:30-33: And Ahab the son of Omri did evil in the sight of the Lord above all that were before him. And it came to pass, as if it had been a light thing for him to walk in the sins of Jeroboam the son of Nebat, that he took to wife Jezebel the daughter of Ethbaal king of the Zidonians, and went and served Baal and worshipped him. And he reared up an altar for Baal in the house of Baal, which he had built in Samaria. And Ahab made a grove; and Ahab did more to provoke the Lord God of Israel to anger than all the kings of Israel that were before him.

Beware of people who have a spirit of control, they are as dangerous as Ahab was. They will monitor your every move; they will become jealous like Saul and try to kill your dreams. They will stop you from learning, in hopes of hindering your growth. You will begin to notice their cooling attitude towards you, and they will operate in the spirit of enmity. The Bible makes it clear that Ahab operated in a spirit of enmity; the spirit of an enemy, both to God and to his people. He openly insulted and offended God by his words and actions, and brought downfall to God's people. Leaders, who contradicts the word of God causes people to have corrupt tendencies of worship. Ahab was afraid God's people would grow spiritually, so he purposely kept them from learning truths, that was liberating.

BEING LED OUT OF SIGHT

After Elijah boldly confronted Ahab, the Lord told Elijah to go to the east and hide by the Cherith Brook at a place east of where it enters the Jordan River. Notice God gave Elijah specific instructions and he obeyed them. In your seasons of confrontation you **MUST** obey God. Your faith in God should especially be alive during this season. Your height of sensitivity in the spirit is very important. You must be able to see and hear very clearly in the spirit because your life may depend upon it. This is not the time you want to be led by a carnal mind or be on an emotional high. You need re-enforced stability in God during your seasons of confrontations. This comes through much praying.

I Kings 17:2-4 (KJV): And the word of the Lord came unto him, staying, Get thee hence, and turn thee eastward, and hide thyself by the brook Cherith, that is before Jordan. And it shall be, that thou shalt drink of the brook; and I have commanded the ravens to feed thee there.

Notice the Lord told Elijah where to go, what to do and what will happen when he gets there. When you obey God by faith, he brings you to a place of total provision, divine restoration and miraculous victory. God also brings you to your place of destiny. Notice, here he enters Jordan River and hide. Israel was a very strong nation politically and militarily. However, they had no spiritual fortress. The Bible makes it clear that Ahab's father Omri during his 12 years rule did not care about Israel's spiritual condition and deliberately led them farther away from God in order to put power in his own hands.

When Omri died, his son Ahab took over and continued the evil reign –like father, like son. To make matters worse, Ahab's evil wife Jezebel who came from the Phoenician City of Tyre, whose father was a high Priest, worshipped Baal in order to please her. Ahab built a temple and an altar for Baal, promoted idolatry, and led the entire nation into sin. Those who worshipped Baal believed that Baal was the god who brought the rain and bountiful harvest. Baal was a god of nature and fertility, whose worship was intended to ensure the rains needed to produce a good crop, so when Elijah confronted Ahab and told him it would not rain for several years, Ahab was shocked. The nation had a strong military defense, but this would be of no help. What they needed was to repent and fall on their faces before the Lord God of Israel. They needed a strong spiritual defense and a strong spiritual leader. When the Spirit of God leads you to boldly confront the evil in today's leaders and the people of God, be prepared also to be led by the Spirit of God into hiding. If God should direct you to go into hiding, do not be presumptuous but follow the Holy Spirit's guide. Remember there is a blessing in your obedience.

BLESSINGS IN OBEDIENCE

Elijah's obedience brought him blessings and caused him to be a blessing. God told Elijah to go eastward to Jordan. The east in general stands for that side of things upon which the rising of the sun gives light. This particular area in biblical history is very significant. In the history of Israel, Jordan is a landmark of great victories. It is the eastern boundaries of biblical Canaan; the promise land. It was where Joshua led the Israelites into Canaan as God miraculously held back the Jordan's water. Significantly, God promised us in Psalms

103:12, when He forgives us, He removes our transgressions "as far as the east is from the west."

1 Kings 17:4, 6-7: And it shall be, that thou shalt drink of the brook; and I have commanded the ravens to feed thee there. And the ravens brought him bread and flesh in the morning, and bread and flesh in the evening; and he drank of the brook. And it came to pass after a while, that the brook dried up, because there had been no rain in the land.

Do not get bent out of shape when the Lord tells you, its time to move from the old dried up place. God has a place where He will send you to experience His providence; He knows exactly what it is going to take for you to fulfill your destiny, so go to the place where you will experience growth. And remember people will not always appreciate the blessing you are or have been, but that is between them and God—just obey God. Do like Elijah did, get up and leave because the brook has dried up.

It is not God's will for His people to be in dry places or to be bound to circumstances, traditions or religion. Being in a dry place and going through the wilderness is not the same, God provided for his people in the wilderness. Ask yourself, "am I growing where I am spiritually?" Even Abram at one point had to come out from among his family to fulfill his destiny. If you are in a place where limitations are set for you to operate within and you know it is not of God, because the brook has dried up, then you are bound.

If you are unable to think for yourself or flow in the purpose of the anointing, then you are bound. My friends, begin to listen to the voice of the Lord for divine direction, and when you hear from the Lord, concerning what to do, have faith and do it. God wants to lead you in the path where the river of His anointing flows, where the living water is, and where your soul can feast on the fatness of the land. A place where the table is spread and there is a feast going on.

There is a real anointing that you can operate in at a place in God, where you can be a tremendous blessing to the Body of Christ, but it takes faith and obedience. There is nothing wrong with boundaries, because there are boundaries set by God for you and I to operate within, however if you are barricaded into wrong doctrines and humanistic beliefs, and the Spirit of Christ is not at liberty to work in your life, that's bondage. Now the Lord is that spirit: and where the Spirit of the Lord is there is liberty (2 Corinthians 3:17). In this Apostolic-prophetic hour that we are living in, we must position ourselves to be used by God. We have destiny to fulfill, we have purpose to produce, we have temples that need to be rebuilt and temple worship that needs to be restored. We do not have as much time as we did yesterday to get back to that place we need to be spiritually. People of God, we are living in that hour of God's manifestation. It is time for the manifestation of the sons of God (Romans 8:19). It is the hour for true sons and spiritual daughters to be revealed. God's creation is waiting; it is standing at attention, with hope and patience of the redemption.

I AM A SURVIVOR

To survive means to remain alive in spite of: In spite of life-threatening accidents. In spite of situations that came to take me out – I outlast it I out lived it. I am still here. There were some dangerous places that I found myself in, but thanks be to God who gives us the victory. Before I got into the accident, before I got into that life-threatening situation, before I entered the danger zone, God already knew that I would make it. He knew that I would survive. He knew that I would weather the storms. God, the All-knowing, All powerful One. He knew that I would remain alive. He knew that I would make it through, my seasons of confrontations. I am a survivor.

Surviving your seasons of confrontations, that appointed or set time of standing and dealing with situations and circumstances in your life will bring about biblical change in you. One of the things we need to understand in our season to endure conflicts and life circumstances, is the importance of our decision to give our lives to Jesus. This is the most significant decision you will ever make in your entire life. Following the path to your destiny and knowing that without Christ, you will never fulfill "who you were destined to be," is your very first step in surviving your season of confrontations.

Do you know that God still hears the Sinner's Prayer? He is waiting for you to come to Him in humble submission so you can survive your storms; try Jesus instead of a bottle of wine, instead of a puff on a cigar, instead of a roll in the hay with someone you don't know by name. Instead of trying to fill a void you desperately hope will go away, a real relationship with Jesus Christ can help you find your way.

Let us pray:

Heavenly Father, I come to you as humble as I know how asking you to come into my heart and fill every empty space. I confess that I have done all that I can to make my life better, but once again I have fallen short. I know that the Bible says for God so love the world, He gave His only begotten Son that whosoever believe in Him should not perish but have everlasting life. I understanding also that Jesus died on the cross so that I might live. I pray now that You will forgive all my sins and grant unto me everlasting life. I come to You now and I accept You as my Heavenly Father. Wash me in Your precious blood and cleanse me from all unrighteousness. Teach me day by day as I commit myself to you, the things I need to know, so that I may live a good Christian life. I receive this new life by faith In Jesus Name, Amen!

CHAPTER 5

AN UNCOMPROMISED STAND

Never compromise the word of God. Always stand on what God says. God Himself will never compromise His word. When you stand on God's Word, stand not by might, nor by power, but by the Spirit of the Lord of Hosts. God is unchangeable; He never makes void His promises.

Numbers 23:19 (KJV): God is not a man that he should lie; neither the son of man that he should repent: hath he said, and shall he not do it? or hath he spoken, and shall he not make it good?

The Lord promises to respond if a widow cries out to Him; He will punish those who harm her; He doth execute the judgement of the fatherless and widow, and loveth the stranger, in giving Him food and raiment. The Psalmist also celebrates God as the one whom "sustains" the fatherless and widow (Deuteronomy 10:18 and Psalm 146:9). After the brook dried up because there was no rain, Elijah was to go on to Zarephath on another assignment.

I Kings 17: 7-9 (KJV): And it came to pass after a while, that the brook dried up, because there had been no rain in the land. And the word of the Lord came unto him, saying, Arise, get thee

to Zarephath, which belongeth to Zion and dwell thee: behold, I have commanded a widow there to sustain thee.

When you are going through your season of conflicts and confrontations, when your personal life and your ministry is under attack, avoid the snare of thinking that you know God so well that you have the 411 on Him. It is not impossible for Him to send the people you least expect to help bring you out of your dry spell. Nor is it impossible that He would allow only certain people to help you. God will prove to man, He is the One who took care of you all along, but you must learn how to trust Him, even when you can't put a finger on exactly what He is doing. Remember your deliverance is not in a person; as much as it is in God. And the person who is sensitive enough to the Holy Spirit, who blesses you, is flowing in the Spirit of Christ as they obey the leading of the Holy Spirit. They are only able to help you because of the God that they serve. The Psalmist says it this way, my help cometh from the Lord who made Heaven and Earth. We must learn how to stand and not compromise in God, no matter how bleak our situation may look. Watch out for temptations in your seasons of conflicts and yield to Holy Ghost Power.

FAITH CHANGES FACTS

Elijah went to Zarephath as the Lord commanded. As he arrived at the gates of the city, the Bible says, he saw a widow woman gathering sticks. Elijah asked the woman for a cup of water. As she was on her way to get the water, Elijah called to her and said bring me a bite to eat, also. The widow turned to the man of God and made an "oath." She said, "I swear as the Lord thy God liveth, I have not a single piece of bread in the house." Little did she know that her miracle was already in the house. It would take her faith to activate the miracle, and bring her the very thing that was already prepared by God for her and her family. Your faith in God's Word and the words spoken by a true Prophet of God can change the facts about whatever you are going through. The widow told Elijah all she had left in her house was a handful of flour in a barrel and a little oil in a cruse, and that she was gathering the sticks to cook this last meal and then both she and her son would wait to die of starvation.

When you are down to your last, do not wait to die, but hope to live, because little can become much when you place it in the Master's hand. God may not come when you want him to, but he will come right on time. Elijah arrived in Zarephath right on time. If there is no need for a miracle in your life, you do not need God to work a miracle. If there is a need for one, have faith that "God can." Things can change and your life is still not revolutionized. That is why you must have faith in God and do not be afraid.

FEAR NOT

When fear tries to take over your life and brings discouragement, rely on the grace of God, plead the blood of Jesus, and remember the mercy of God that brought you thus far. Greater is He that is in you, than he that is in the world. Do not die in the wilderness of life. God has promised in His word never to leave you or forsake you, cast all your cares upon Him, He cares for you.

I Kings 17:13-16 (KJV): And Elijah said unto her, Fear not; go and do as thou has said: but make me thereof a little cake first, and bring it unto me, and after make for thee and for thy son. For thus saith the Lord God of Israel, The barrel of meal shall not waste, neither shall the cruse of oil fail, until the day that the Lord sendeth rain upon the earth. And she went and did according to the saying of Elijah: and she, and he, and her house, did eat many days. And the barrel of meal wasted not, neither did the cruse of oil fail, according to the word of the Lord, which he spake by Elijah.

You are only afraid of what you see, when your faith cannot witness the spiritual evidence of all that God is doing through the circumstances you are facing. Your faith only gives evidence to things that are unseen. The widow woman did not even consider that God was able to deliver her from this famine. She was preparing herself and her son to die after they had eaten their last meal, so to speak. She spoke death into her child's life even before he was actually troubled by the spirit of death. When your faith is alive you speak life, if you waiver in your faith, you will speak death, but thanks be to God who has given us the victory. Could it be that the seed of death entered the life of the boy, when the Mother spoke of her preparing their last meal so that they might eat and then wait to die?

I Kings 17:17, 20 & 22 (KJV): And it came to pass after these things, that the son of the woman, the mistress of the house, fell sick; and his sickness was so sore, that there was no breath left in him. And he (Elijah) cried unto the Lord, and said, O Lord my God, hast thou also brought evil upon the widow with whom I sojourn, by slaying her son? And the Lord heard the voice of Elijah; and the soul of the child came into him again, and he revived.

Some people know the word of God, but they miss what it means. With man this is impossible but with God ALL things are possible. Be confident that God cares for His own and will deliver in times of disaster. Do not be afraid of the circumstances of life, instead fear the Living God, and make a fresh commitment to trust Him. Through trust in God, we gain the victory.

FAITH THAT REVOLUTIONIZES

Elijah lived in critical times; Israel needed a spiritual revolution. After his initial meeting with Ahab, God sent him to the place where he would ultimately experience victory. He came to the pinnacle of his ministry and the place of every Christian's dream of being caught up into the heavens. Elijah would later pass over the Jordan into a wilderness area where God would transport Elijah up to heaven. Three years later the Lord said to Elijah...Go tell king Ahab that I will soon send rain again, so Elijah went to tell him. Meanwhile, the famine had become very severe in Samaria. While Elijah was on his way to see Ahab, the same day Ahab said unto Obadiah, we must go into all the land to see if we can find enough grass to save at least some of my horses and mules. Obadiah was a man that feared the Lord. Obadiah and Ahab went separate ways to search the entire land (1 Kings 18).

All of a sudden Obadiah saw Elijah coming towards him. Obadiah bowed down to the ground and said to Elijah, "is it really you, my lord Elijah?" Elijah replied, "it is, go tell your master I am here."

Obadiah protested, as surely as the Lord your God lives, there is not a nation or kingdom where my master has not sent someone to look for you. And whenever a nation or kingdom claimed you were not there, he made the king of that nation take "oath" and swear to the truth of his claim. I do not know where the Spirit of the Lord may carry you when I leave you; if I go and tell Ahab and he does not find you he will kill me.

When God tells you to go show yourself to the enemy, do not be afraid; do not let your heart become troubled. But trust in the Lord with all your heart and do not lean to your own flesh, or carnal ways, (Proverb. 3:5-6) your flesh cannot revolutionize your life, but your faith can. Acknowledge your God and watch Him fulfill His promises to you, His servant. Not only will God fulfill His promises; He will also direct your path. God will give you a testimony if you trust in him and do not be afraid. Be faithful and declare to the enemy, "I SHALL NOT BE MOVED", and just watch God establish you in faith that will remain alive yet unshakable.

Elijah assures Obadiah that he will show himself to the King. When the king saw Elijah, he said, "is that you who troubleth Israel?" Men and women who stand for what they know is right and that which is in accordance to the word of God are often called troublemakers. Real troublemakers however, are those who think they are right, know they are actually wrong and will not repent. They cause trouble to the righteous. Repentance brings revival in our personal walk with God. When you and I allow God to use us, He will revolutionize our minds and hearts, our faith will become alive and we will become unmovable in our faith. The Bible says, many are called but few are chosen. I believe you must do something different from all the called out ones if you want to be among the chosen. How do we know that you are chosen? By your acts of obedience. The chosen will always obey God; beyond their understanding, imagination or feelings. Do not think for one second that you don't have to do anything, because you are chosen anyway. If you are indeed chosen, why are you afraid to obey God?

If you are going to heaven anyway, why are you afraid to live with Him, here today (1 Peter 1:2)?

To avoid living a compromised Christian life you must have faith in spite of what comes your way. We certainly do not change our minds about our natural fathers, when things don't go our way. Likewise, you cannot change your mind about God because of life's challenges. Our faith becomes an in spite of faith, when we are able to stand on the word of God, even in the face of adversity and go through. Our God is a faithful God, He will not allow us to be tempted beyond our capacity to overcome; He strengthens and protects us from the evil one so we can celebrate the faithfulness of our God.

Psalm 89:1-2 (KJV): I will sing of the mercies of the Lord for ever: with my mouth will I make known thy faithfulness to all generations. For I have said, Mercy shall be built up for ever; thy faithfulness shall thou establish in the very heavens.

You must believe that the Lord is able to establish you in faithfulness and righteousness. And if you can understand the depth of God's love for you and believe that He will not change his mind concerning you, guess what? It will be easier for you to tap into the realm of the Spirit that will revolutionize your life forever.

SURVIVAL OF THE FITTEST

This is our season, but seasons, set and appointed times does not come without conflicts and confrontations that must be endured. It is not right for us to believe because we are blessed, we will never see trouble or because we have trouble in our lives, we have done something wrong. Let your faith be one that is alive and unshakable. I am beginning to realize more and more that we cannot survive confrontations and the conflicts of life without obedience to the will of God. To survive we must put up a fight to stay not only in the will of God, but we must also fight to stay away from compromising God's word, which is His guidelines and rules.

God requires obedience from His people and we are very precious to Him. He wants our allegiance. It is important to Him that we take the right path. Taking the right path ensures our survival. **Psalms 119:105 says: Thy word is a lamp unto my feet, and a light unto my path.** We live in a world full of darkness, a world that has turned its back on God. A world filled with chaos, confusion, and poverty. Without the light of the world we will never make it. Jesus said to His disciples **"As long as I am in the world, I am the light of the word."** (John 9:5 (KJV)) Can you imagine being in this world without Jesus?

The Bible gives us our basic instructions for living a "Blessed" life right here on this Earth. We are the survivors. One of my favorite lessons to teach to my disciples as a Christian leader is to "stay focused." I realize that most of us get off track because of a lack of focus. Generally, if we can stay focused, on our vision for life we can endure just about anything that comes our way. People who stay focused on the vision are motivated when all hell breaks loose because the revelation in their hearts is, "I trust God as my source and power and I can always count on Him." Trusting God increases your greatness in Him.

It doesn't matter who your Mama is, or daddy, they do not have the power to increase your greatness, nor do they possess the ability to comfort you on every side. For some of us, our parents could not even control us, their ability was limited against our will, but nevertheless, God always gets His way. Many of us do not know how to handle confrontation, because our parents were afraid of confrontation themselves. We have become products of our environment and households, even our neighborhoods, our cultural and geographical locations –can anything good come out of Nazareth? You'll be surprised.

The spirit of confrontation rears its ugly head all the time in children, who whine, fuss and throw temper tantrums, for a piece of candy instead of a bottle of milk. And because of the fear of being embarrassed, parents will give in, because by nature some are trained to be timid. This made many stubborn, rather than submissive, screaming for attention and withdrawn when things do not go their way. It is by faith that we are able to survive seasons of conflict. If God can take a formless Earth and make it livable, He can take your life and equip you so that you become fit to survive. Thank God He is not intimidated by this godless society.

Seek Righteousness

We must come to realize more than ever before, that we need God. It is time to seek righteousness and humility. It is time to listen and heed the voice of God. I submit to you my Brothers and Sisters in the Lord, that God wants to promote you. Yes, it's a prominent place, but it is not a pedal stool. Promotion comes from God not from the east, nor the west, nor from the south. There is a set time for God to lift you up and trust me you do not want to miss the season of God for your life. *For the wise shall inherit glory but shame shall be the promotion of fools.* It's amazing to me how people are sometime afraid of being used and promoted by God, because they lack responsibility and accountability; but sometimes they end up promoting themselves anyway. The very ones who were once afraid are no longer fearful when they realize what God can do in them. And as soon as they get wind of what they are capable of doing in God, they become exalted in themselves and forget their humiliation. I admonish you, seek righteousness.

Let me speak to those of you who are afraid that you might be accused of exalting yourselves. Many of you failed in your lack of understanding. What some of you failed to realize is that you have been chosen before the foundation of the world. The Bible says to be holy and without blame (Ephesian 1:4). We are a chosen people, a people of excellence carefully selected by God to lift up the Son of God. As a leader, I have seen people whom God desires to use to build the kingdom of God, who were afraid to go forth and once they went forth and realized the wealth of their calling, they begin to lose focus. Instead of seeking after righteousness they begin to exalt their gift, thus failing to remain in an uncompromised stand, they fall by the wayside. There are others on the other hand they cannot see themselves, the way God sees them, they submit to me that they don't have anything to offer. I encourage you –you may not see yourself as special, but God thinks that you are special.

John 15:16 (KJV) says: Ye have not chosen me, but I have chosen you, and ordained you, that ye should go and bring forth fruit, and that your fruit should remain: that whatsoever ye shall ask of the Father in my name, he may give it you.

God could have rejected you, but instead he chose you and gave you favor. I don't think that's a bad thing at all. The Spirit of the Lord chose you a long time ago, and set you aside from that which is common, and usual, and He gave you the characteristics of God. That is why you are so different, you have always been different. You have been called and chosen to seek after righteousness. Raising your standards is also a part of seeking righteousness. Standards are something set up as a rule or model with which other things like it are compared. They are rules we govern our lives by. So, why do we need rules or yet to raise our standards, because God says so.

CHAPTER 6

SEASONS OF PROMOTION

We live in a season of outpouring. A day and time in which God wants to bless us. He wants to release deliverance in the lives of his people and shower down upon us favor that is beyond our imagination. I believe that God's desire is to make Himself known to His people in a way that is undeniable. The gift of God is being stirred in those of us that have chosen to become fit for the Master's use. I have a burning desire to see souls rescued from hell. I want to experience the supernatural in my day. I want to see miracles, and I know that it will happen in my time, my generation and in my seasons of promotion.

John 14:12 (KJV) says: Verily, verily I say unto you, He that believeth on me, the works that I do shall he do also: and greater works than these shall he do; because I go unto my Father.

This greater outpouring of God's Spirit being release in the Earth realm is for the benefit of God's people. When I see young people working for the Lord in an anointing that I did not realize was available to me when I was their age, that alone is a miracle to me. When I see what I believe is a "remnant" that God is raising up and setting apart for his purpose, who is excited about God I get excited too. Young Apostolic-prophetic people, self-assured and confident that God has called them, and giving God the glory can give you a sense of hope, in this dark and dying world. Jesus said "I have chosen you and ordained you." Being ordained means that you have been reserved, you have been appointed and set aside for God's purpose.

I remember having a dream one night about a three-year-old child that use to attend our church, God showed me in the dream our congregation worshipping so intensely that the anointing fell even on the children. The anointing was so potent and powerful you could literally feel the weight of His glory in the sanctuary and this child was worshipping the Lord with hands lifted up and tears rolling down her face. In the dream she appeared to be about seven or eight. I would often say when the children become eight and ten years old, people will come to our church just to hear them pray, preach and worship the Lord. I dedicate myself to praying for the younger generation, because God always dealt with me as a "Spiritual Father" in ministry. God has been preparing me for a long time as an "Apostolic Leader," therefore my dedication to God and my devotion to His people, is to teach and train in such a way. There will be a generation preserved to receive a spiritual inheritance.

I long to see true spiritual sons and daughters raised up by God in such a way that when my time comes to step aside, and allow my spiritual children to begin operating in a greater outpouring of apostolic-prophetic anointing. I will be persuaded that they are empowered by God, and the counsel they received from me as their spiritual leader, will enable them to trust and obey the commands of God better than their teacher.

I believe in the promise of God that in the last days His spirit will be poured out upon all flesh (Acts 2:17; Joel 2:28). I believe if our children can carry guns to school at eight years old, they are not too young to learn the Bible.

Do you realize that right here in America there are elementary and middle schools that installs metal detectors, because our kids are bringing guns and knives to school. If they are becoming drugs dealers by the time they are twelve, and having sex at fifteen years old, then they are not too young to preach and teach the word of God, as far as I'm concerned, they are not too young to pray and intercede for themselves and on behalf of others. I believe in teaching them at an early age how to be servants in the Lord's Church. I believe in protecting them in prayer. If at six years old they know every song on the radio, and music videos, they know how to turn the TV to BET, they know who Beyonce, Ludacris, and Jay-Z are, then they should also know Matthew, Mark, Luke, John, and who Jesus is. After all these are Christian kids. And since they can remember every Rapper and every rap song then I am a believer that they can also remember "the armor of God" so why not teach it to them now, while their minds are still shapeable. I believe in our children, they are our future.

The Bible says God has chosen and ordained you to bring forth fruit –to bring forth the visible expression of power working inwardly so that the invisible power of the Holy Ghost in those who are brought into living union with Christ will be evident in our character. When we allow God to shape and mold us, there would be such a unity of the character and integrity of God produced in us that the fruit of the spirit will be evident and that's when you are ready for promotion. That's when you are ready for the next assignment.

The Bible says the fruit of the Spirit is love, joy, peace, longsuffering, kindness, goodness, faithfulness, meekness and temperance. And when these become visible outward manifestations of the power of God working in you, you are ready to be used by God. You are now in position to let your guards down and trust God to be your lifeguard. You are now ready to launch out into the deep, because you are equipped with the evidence that the power of God is at work in your life.

In your season of promotion you must be at peace with yourself and with God. Allowing God to work on you will impact your daily lives as well as your destiny. In our seasons of confrontation we must win the war within. God often places us in situations so that we might overcome our inner struggles. If we refuse to allow God to work on us before we come to this point in our spiritual walk, while God is trying to take us to the next dimension in the Spirit, we will continue to stumble and we may even fall.

Psalms 119:165-AMP says: Great peace have they who love Your law; nothing shall offend them or make them stumble.

The Bible also says; that the work of righteousness is peace and the effects is quietness and assurance. If we do not walk in peace in our seasons of promotion, we will walk in the shadows of other people rather than in the spirit and power of God. Walking in the shadows of others will hinder you from coming into the fullness of who you really are in Christ Jesus.

God's Divine Power

In our seasons of promotion we must know how to recognize as well as interpret what the Lord is doing in our lives the proper way. If we can recognize and interpret the moves of God properly. We will know that it is on God's divine power alone we must depend. In our seasons of promotion, depending on divine power will help you to accomplish God's purposes.

Isaiah 1:3 (NKJV) says: The ox knows its owner And the donkey its master's crib; But Israel does not know, My people do not consider.

What is God saying about his people in this passage of scripture: He says the ox and the donkey intuitively know the object they depend upon. They perceive immediately their provision and they receive immediate insight, understanding or inspiration of who their provider is. In other words God says about the ox and the donkey that they possess the kind of characteristics or perception without conscious reasoning that the owner is provider and the master's crib is provision. God says here my people Israel does not know its owner and even though they are God's people, chosen to receive an inheritance from God, they do not consider God's Provision.

In our seasons of promotion God also allows us to go through seasons of elimination, which confronts inner struggles that hinders us from receiving the greater anointing. Seasons of elimination prunes us, and purges us, and removes from us those things that gets in the way of God empowering us for our next level of promotion.

In our seasons of promotion we must be careful not to move out of the plan and purpose of God for our lives. As long as you are growing and maturing in Christ Jesus, He will elevate you in the Spirit. This does not necessarily mean in title or even in some specialize position, but you may become more knowledgeable of the things of God and He will take you to the next dimension in the spirit. This is the very reason why we must depend on His divine power to accomplish the task God has prepared for us. The enemy of our soul seeking to destroy God's plan for our lives will come with his gimmicks and games, and if you are not careful, you will find yourself making premature moves, just to get God to elevate you.

It is God's desire that we have a future with a hope and when we depend on His divine power, His purpose and plans for our lives will be accomplished. For I know the plans I have for you says the Lord, plans for good and not for disaster, to give you a future and a hope - in those days when you pray I will listen (Jeremiah 29). God has great plans for His people and as soon as you make up in your mind to follow His plans for your life; in those days when you pray. God will listen. God wants to empower us so that we may accomplish His purpose in the future. He is ready to open doors and release great things in our lives. This is our receiving day, a day of overflowing blessings and great abundance. Remember God's plan is not for disaster, but hope for the future.

God's divine power is a creative power. In the beginning God created the heavens and the Earth and the Earth was without form and void and the Bible says God spoke and out of His divine power He created something out of nothing. Should we try to create something out of nothing all we would get is confusion, but not God. Out of nothingness, emptiness, and formlessness, he makes something of worth.

Job 26:7 (KJV) says: He stretcheth out the north over the empty place, and hangeth the earth upon nothing.

In ages past He laid the foundation of the earth and the heavens are the work of His hands. To depend on God's divine power to accomplish His purpose; God's purpose must also be your purpose. It is God's purpose to place you in a position to possess the promise. A position is a place occupied by a person. It can also be an attitude, a point of view, a class or rank. When God places a person in position, He expects them to take a stance and to be in the right attitude of mind. If we do not possess the mind of Christ it will be difficult for us to possess the right attitude of mind. Without the right attitude of mind, a person can easily loose hope, forget what God had promised, and become discouraged and easily hindered when they come up against opposition. A person can also become disillusioned if they do not possess the right attitude of mind.

Philippians 2:5 (KJV) says: Let this mind be in you, which was also in Christ Jesus.

Jesus is our example and the Bible says that we should follow in His steps. We must understand that Jesus without ceasing to be God became human, so that we may have a high priest who can be touched by our infirmities. Jesus knows who we are and He can identify with what we are going through at all times. On your way to the top, be careful that you do not become self-serving, but let the mind of Christ be in you and the word of God dwell richly in your heart. Don't live only to make a good impression on other people or just to please yourself, this is not a good way of living for the Christian, this is a self-centered living.

Don't Be Selfish

Believers should have the kind of attitude that will make them give up their "rights" for the good of others. As a Prophetic leader I have been exposed to people's selfishness, pride and evil. Because they held on to their rights when wronged, their privileges to control their own lives and their position which was granted to them by the grace of God through their spiritual leader. People who toy with ideas of spiritual murder and the abortion of their unborn child. Those who had deliberately plan the demise of others. There are those who remain in evil relationships outside the covenant of marriage. Those who marry hoping to get rid of their whorish ways and the ones who held on to their pride and promoted evil, even in the House of God, because they stake claim that they are equal to their spiritual leaders. This is the hour for true worship, don't be selfish in your ways.

Notice in John 1:1 Jesus is equal to God, because He is God. But even Jesus voluntarily gave up His divine rights, and His position in glory, because of His love for the Father. Jesus' claim was "My doctrine is not mine, but His that sent me." (John 6:17) Jesus is the One who should be in control of our lives. If you are honest, you will admit that when you were in control of your life, you did a lousy job. You cheated on your taxes, because you felt you deserve to have more money. You may have aborted a baby, because you felt you had the right to control your own body. You went wherever you wanted to, did whatsoever pleased you, all because you wanted to hold on to what you believe were your rights, privileges and your position in life. As believers however, we should have the right attitude of mind. God has called us as servants and when we develop a servant's heart, we will learn how to serve one another with dignity, for the sake of building up the Body of Christ and the House of the Lord.

Jesus was God, but He humbled Himself so that He may willfully obey God and serve His people. When we give up our rights and humble ourselves, we will serve God out of love for Him and for others. **John 3:16 (KJV) says: For God so loved the world that he gave his only begotten Son, that whosoever believeth in him should not perish but have everlasting life.**

God proves to us here that there is true love, you can truly love someone in such a way that you are willing to lay down your life for him or her. Only God can do this in us. There is no selfishness in this kind of love. For those of you who have been wondering if something is wrong with you, because you love your spiritual leaders, your brothers and sisters in the Lord, nothing is wrong with you, you simply love the Lord and his people. On the contrary something is right about you. Because of Jesus we can genuinely love one another, care for one another and protect each other. That is pure love, genuine and without hatred, jealousy and malice.

Love heals, while selfishness only makes you miserable. When you live life selfishly as a Christian, you make choices as though this life is all we have. But notice in John 3:16, we are promised everlasting life. Pure love is not self-centered, but self-sacrificing and willingness to give freely what is true love. That is why God gave his Son, it was an act of self-sacrifice.

In your seasons of promotion stay clear of selfishness. The same God that gave is the same God that can take away. The Bible says, to whom much is given much is required. **Luke 12:48 (TLB): But anyone who is not aware that he is doing wrong will be punished only lightly. Much is required from those to whom much is given, for their responsibility is greater.**

God is calling his people to be sincere. He is calling us to properly relate to one another. We are living as I stated before, in an Apostolic-prophetic hour and we have been given the opportunity by God to live out our Faith. When the outward manifestations of our belief becomes evident in our lives, as Children of God, we will reflect the love of Jesus as we relate to one another. John 13:35 says: By this shall men know that ye are my disciples, if ye have love one to another. God is calling us to be sincere in our relationships to one another. Not hypocritical, anxious, lazy, greedy and fearful, but trustworthy, generous, sincere and full of faith, that is alive and unshakable.

Jesus promises to reward those who are faithful to the Master. Although God never lies and enjoys blessing us for our faithfulness, many in the Body of Christ deny themselves the joy of serving the Lord diligently, because they foolishly expect material rewards for every faithful act they complete. What God has in store for us, far out weight any material reward. Yes, God will reward you materially, but please do not limit your rewards to the material realm only. Like Esau, you may forfeit your birthright, or like Absalom, you may devise some wicked scheme of rebellion, or like Achan you may cause the demise of your entire family, by underestimating God.

Love is an attitude that will reveal itself in action. How can we love someone and at the same time, act selfishly towards them –we can't. That is the reason why people sometimes misinterpret love, especially true love which can be interpreted as tough love at times. Only because of pure love will you be able to receive someone, without malice in your heart after they seek to destroy you. What a mighty God we serve. How can we love as Christ loves? By loving when it is not convenient for us.

The Bible says love covers a multitude of sins. I remember allowing someone to live with me at one time, whom I was warned will hurt me. I was not as concerned about being hurt as I was about the Christians who were upset, because they had a problem with me helping another saint. Where is the love? Can you give love even when it hurts? Can you help someone when it is not convenient for you? Can you devote your time and energy towards someone else's welfare, when their so-called friends say to you, they will turn around and hurt you? The Bible says love knows no ill, so even if it's true, why not be a real Christian and show some love? My love for God and His people will not allow me to be afraid of being hurt. Love cast out all fears.

Love Is An Attitude

When the Spirit of God Himself lives in you, you will be able to do things you deem impossible. Before you become a born again believer, you may have been able to hate someone that wronged you, but when you become born again, it is absolutely impossible for you to hate someone. **Leviticus 19:17a says: Thou shalt not hate thy brother in thine heart;** Jesus told us to love the Lord with all our hearts and our neighbor as ourselves. This is God's command and if we truly love God, we will keep His law.

Love is an attitude. The Bible says: why call me Lord, Lord and do not the things that I say. I encourage you to begin concentrating on what you can do to keep God's command. Let us show God how much we love Him and others.

2 Corinthians 5:17 (KJV) says: Therefore if any man be in Christ, he is a new creature: old things are passed away; behold, all things are become new.

When you become a Christian, according to the Word of God, you become a brand new person. The Holy Spirit is the one that gives us *new life,* and our new life comes from within, therefore we are no longer the same. Greater is He that is in me *now,* than he that is in the world. Our attitude should be different because we now have a brand new Master, so the things we use to do, we don't do anymore. Some of the places we use to go, we cannot go there any longer, and some of the people we use to hang with, we don't hang with any more. At least not until we have grown enough in Christ, where they can no longer influence us to live the old life. But when we can spiritually impact their old life, by the transformed life, we now live.

You are no longer a sinner, so the life you now live, you live as though you are a brand new creature. If you had a problem with hate, jealousy, pride, whatever sin's that may have plagued your life, before you became a Christian, you must believe by faith that God is able to deliver you. If you had a bad attitude; and everyone knew you as such, when you become rooted in and connected to Christ, as your new Master, He will give you strength to submit your will to Him and you can now learn how to live with the right attitude of mind. But if you do not fully submit your will to the Master, so you can draw life and strength from Him, you are in danger of being fooled. You may believe a lie, thinking it's the truth if you are not totally submitted to Christ.

You also need to be part of a Bible believing, Bible teaching Church, where you can learn and grow in God. I would also like to add finding a Church where the gifts of the Spirit are in operation is a good choice. If you are convicted by the preached word that is a good sign, also that you are in the right place. If you feel compelled to pursue holiness you are in the right place. Conviction is not to make you feel bad, it's to make you change. Remember, you are now a new creature. So out with the old, and in with the new.

When God begins to take you to new heights in Him, you may be tempted to change your attitude from true humility to false humility. Be careful that you do not become ensnared. Before we believed in Christ our nature was evil. Now that we are in Christ, we contend with the evil in this world, because the enemy of our soul wars against us for the affection of our Lord and Savior. God has placed some of you in position, just where He wants you to be, so He can get the best out of you. Some of you, He has positioned you for your next level of promotion. Joshua was such a one, he was placed in position to fill Moses' shoes. God positioned Moses to lead His people, Moses shepherded the people of God until His death. Then the Bible says; After the death of Moses God's servant, the Lord spoke to Joshua who was Moses's assistant and He said: Now that Moses my servant is dead you must lead my people across the Jordan River into the land I am giving them (Joshua 1). One version says; God told Joshua to arise. Because I promise you what I promised Moses. (Read Joshua 1:1-9) Did you notice, God did not ask Joshua if he wanted this assignment? God simply appointed him. **Numbers 27:15-18 says: And Moses spake unto the Lord,**

saying, Let the Lord, the God of the spirits of all fresh, set a man over the congregation. Which may go out before them, and which may go in before them, and which may lead them out, and which may bring them in; that the congregation of the Lord be not as sheep which have no shepherd. And the Lord said unto Moses, Take thee Joshua the son of Nun, a man in whom is the spirit, and lay thine hand upon him;

Joshua had assisted Moses for thirty-nine years, so he was well prepared to take over the leadership of the nation. New leaders must be trained for their responsibility in case they are promoted to ensure God's House can continue to operate effectively. One of the things we experience in the House of God in this Apostolic-prophetic era, is the lack of respect Church leaders have, when it comes to the responsibility they have been given to build up the House of God. Remember, when I speak of leadership, I speak of all church staff, intercessors and deacons. For example when I was coming up in my early years in ministry, I had a sense of responsibility and honor for the position that I held in the House of God. Quite naturally, today I have a greater sense of responsibility and honor. What I see today, is, people who leave their stations or positions in the House of God, with no one else occupying their places. They seem to think that it is ok to make those decisions for God.

In the armed forces, if a soldier leaves his or her post before their duty is over, that would be negligent. He or she can face serious consequences. A soldier is trained to never leave his or her post unattended for any reason, but to make sure the post is secured at all times and especially before going off duty. It has always been my experience that when God was preparing me for a new position, He always allowed me to train someone else to take my place.

God is a God of order. What works in the natural Army also works in the Army of the Lord. The correct way to do this would be to go to my immediate leader first; if I reported to a team or auxiliary leader, or I would go directly to my Pastor, the Shepherd or Overseer of the congregation. Always make sure you follow proper spiritual protocol, so that you receive God's blessing and the proper counsel you need to ensure that you are in the will and season of God for your life. Sometimes people leave churches prematurely. If you have a team or auxiliary leader, it is "right" to speak with them first so they won't be in the dark, before you go to other members of the congregation. Whether your intent is to hurt someone or not, whenever you leave a position in your church, out of order as a leader; because you have built covenant relationships with others, they will be hurt, especially if you are out of God's timing. God has a way of preparing people for what is to come and you can always keep your godly relationships and friendships, when things are done in decency and in order. God will prepare the people around you and no one will backslide and fall away from the things of God, when you move according to his timing.

As Godly leaders we must operate in a true spirit and attitude of love, lest someone's blood be on our hands. If you report directly to your Pastor, it is a good idea to speak with him or her first. Make an appointment and take with you the name of the person you recommend as your successor, this is the person you know can no doubt take your place. You have already prayed, you know the character of this person, and you have received word from the Lord. Your Pastor will confirm what the Lord has spoken to you, because as your leader he or she hears from God concerning your life and destiny. When Moses prayed God told him to take Joshua and guess what, Joshua had no say in it, but he chose to obey God through Moses. If your Pastor releases you, make sure you complete the process by writing a letter of resignation to the church and also to your auxiliary if you serve in one. And if necessary, receive a letter of recommendation and release to your next church home; close the doors properly and receive the blessings of the Lord to continue the work of God in another pasture.

If you do not leave in order, it would be as though you left out of the back doors of the church, only thieves and robbers leave out of God's vineyard through the backdoor method. Should your

Pastor tell you not yet; stay and remain faithful to the work of the Lord, with the right attitude of mind. God will bless you for your obedience and when your Pastor does release you, you will be released with a double portion anointing to operate in your calling. Joshua was Moses' assistant for 39 years. God honored him, in his place of preparation and obedience. He followed God and God gave him success. He was placed in position to possess the promise.

Numbers 27:18-20, 22-23: And the Lord said unto Moses, Take thee Joshua the son of Nun, a man in whom is the spirit, and lay thine hand upon him; And set him before Eleazar the priest, and before all the congregation; and give him a charge in their sight. And thou shalt put some of thine honor upon him, that all the congregation of the children of Israel may be obedient. And Moses did as the Lord commanded him: and he took Joshua, and set him before Eleazar the priest, and before all the congregation: And he laid his hands upon him, and gave him a charge, as the Lord commanded by the hand of Moses.

Divine Authority and Dominion

Moses showed signs of a true "Spiritual Father," he did not want to leave the work God gave him, until a new leader had been trained to replace him. When Joshua was appointed, Moses gave him assignments that helped him become more effective in his new position. Joshua was given divine authority and dominion by the laying on of hands by Moses. Moses also told the people that Joshua had the authority, the ability, and dominion to handle the job to lead the people. A common mistake that young leaders in training make, is thinking that the people are following them because they are more anointed than the leader who asked God to appoint them to the position, in the first place. The only reason why they followed you is because your "Spiritual Father" validated you.

When you have been blessed with a leader who has confidence in you, don't take the authority they've given to you for granted, and start an uprising in your church. God considers this rebellion. People who commit such acts are operating in the spirit of Absalom and they need to repent to God and those leaders they have wronged. Because of people like yourselves, leaders are sometimes afraid of trusting and having confidence in others. Most young leaders do not understand the principle of avoiding "leadership gaps" in our churches. If you understood this principle, you would have never done what you did. A leadership gap takes place when there is no one in the church who is capable of leading the people, besides the Pastor. If you are privileged to be a part of a church where you are operating in your calling, and have found favor with your pastor, you must guard your heart. Pastors need people who are willing to become Joshua.

Are you aware of how many churches are sometimes left without a Joshua if the Pastor dies, or has to leave suddenly or takes sick, and has to be hospitalized. It is important for "Spiritual Fathers" to train a successor, but it's hard to find a Joshua, these days. People are not as dedicated to the Lord's work as before. I randomly asked some people that go to church, how long they've been in their current churches and it is amazing how often people change church these days. Many of the people attended at least three churches within the last five years. There is no way a person can get rooted in and connected to God, going from church to church. It is rear to stay in one church for a period of ten years in the era we now live in, much less serving under a leader for thirty-nine years, which Joshua did. If you have been in your church for any length of time and you are determined to stay there until God completes the work in you, you are to be commended. It takes a lot of endurance to overcome persecution in your season of promotion.

Before God elevates us, we usually go through a period of persecution and betrayal. More often than not, people are unable to endure these periods in their lives. They go from church to church to void the process God takes them through, and the pressure and persecution they receive from people who may simply be jealous of them. If you allow God to shape and mold you, your faith will become alive and unshakable. And like David you will receive power to overcome every Saul you must face, before God takes you to your next level of promotion.

Moses is the one who asked God to appoint a leader who was bold, courageous and had the caring, qualities that he himself possessed. Moses cared about the people, so quite naturally he would pray for a leader who would also care for the people. A good leader cares about goals, but they care more about the peoples' souls. They care that the people are saved and that they are protected. Young leaders in training must be careful to be influenced by the discerner or the power of God's word. And not good sounding words by people who wish to take their places. There are so many Christians today who are messed up, because they do not understand the power in being influenced by the right words. When you are hungry for your life to be shaped, by good sounding words, you will most definitely be messed up, if God's word comes as a crushing hammer or a devouring fire (Jeremiah 5:14). In your seasons of promotion always remember that godliness is better than giftedness. Seek to be godly, let the word of God abide in your heart and let your faith come alive.

God gives us strength to endure during difficult times. He wants us empowered for His purpose. Giving us divine authority and dominion in the earth realm, is God's way of advancing the Kingdom of God in these evil days. **Romans 12:21 says: Be not overcome of evil, but overcome evil with good.** When we accept the place in which God has planted us, we are in the process of fulfilling our God-given purpose. As we bring forth the fruit of our ministry, we must be mindful that God wants us to have the right attitude of mind. Keep in mind the enemy does not want us in place to possess the promises of God, so he (Satan) will have us focus on the pressures of life, but God is looking for us to put into action his Word (Psalm 34:19). Enduring soundness and walking in faith is the key to overcoming the enemy (Hebrews 11:1,3,6). Some people think if they stay in the safety zone of being passive and timid, God will understand. But this is your season to possess your promise, and sound teaching will help you understand that (2 Timothy 1:7). Staying humble while you operate in the Spirit of Christ and soundness of mind will help you to develop an unshakable faith. The kind of faith that is "ALIVE" and will cause you to be unmovable.

PRAYER OF RELEASE

Father in the Name of Jesus, according to the commission you have given unto me. And according to the authority you have invested in me. I now take authority over the lives of your people and release unto them the ability of the great commission. I release the miracle anointing upon them to receive the impossible. I release the power of the Almighty into their hands. Father, let the apostolic and the prophetic power to do end time Ministry, be released into their lives for great influence on those that need repentance in Jesus Name. I release the gifts of healing, the working of miracles and unshakable faith to them in Jesus' Mighty Name.

Lord you said in Your word that the harvest is ripe but the laborers are few. I release to your people the courage to labor and bring forth the fruit of the harvest. Holy Spirit, go with them now, guide and counsel them. Teach them each day how to grow in their own ministries, and how to be faithful in the vineyard they are assigned to, let them become everything you divinely designed them to be. Lord, give them a quick return on the investments they have made into your kingdom. Let this prayer bear witness of the word You have breathe over them, as they daily apply the word of God and godly principles to their lives.

Father, You said Your heart is grieved, because when You look at the lost generations and the multitude of people, there is not enough laborers. Anoint Your people with hearts of compassion for the lost in Jesus Name. We dress ourselves now, with the whole armor of God as we go forth to reap the harvest. Our loins are girt about with truth, we have on the breastplate of righteousness. Our feet are shod with the preparation of the gospel of peace. Above all we take the shield of faith wherewith we quench all the fiery darts of the wicked one, we put on the helmet of salvation. And we take in our hands the sword of the spirit which is the word of God. Now that we are ready and armed, we declare that we are fully equipped to go forth and take the world for the kingdom of God.

Today, Lord and Master, our hearts says "yes" to Your will, and to Your way. We decree and declare that we can do it. We are not going to hold back anymore, but we are going to move out in the name of Jesus and witness to the lost. We are a part of God's great army, and we have all the power we need right now to be soul winners in Jesus Name. Amen!

BIOGRAPHY

Apostle Elene Nicholas is an anointed woman of God, an entrepreneur, songwriter, and a modern day, renaissance woman. Ordained as a Chief Elder and set in position as Overseer in the office of "Apostle" November 2001, by Bishop Rodney S. Walker of God is in Control Church, Waldorf, Maryland. She carries the apostolic mantle well, by seeking to maintain biblical order without being bias, and by operating in the spirit and power of prayer, and a pure love towards all people. She served the Body of Christ in a Pastorate position for eleven years and as Overseer of five Churches within the Washington, DC Metropolitan area for approximately six years until December 2010, under the leadership of Bishop David G. Evans, Abundant Harvest Fellowship of Churches, Lindenwold, New Jersey. She is a product of Greater Mount Calvary Holy Church, in Washington DC, where Bishop Alfred A. Owens and Co-Pastor Susie C. Owens' teaching and training significantly impacts the order in which she functions in ministry, and is reflected and evident in the way she governs and conduct the work of ministry today.

She currently serves as CEO of Erlene Nicholas Global Ministries, and Overseer at THE PRAYER SQUAD a Virtual Christian Community, and Online Apostolic Training Platform.

Lady E. as she is affectionally known throughout her community and among friends, loves the Lord with all her heart. She has a passion for prayer and worship, and she is a radical prayer warrior who has dedicated her life to teaching, training and equipping believers globally, encouraging them to reap the end time harvest, sharpening them in the word of God, and in their gift of intercession. God has truly anointed her with His divine grace and favor and the "Hand" of the Lord are evident upon her life as she walks in the spirit of humility. She has been preaching the gospel for over 30 years, throughout the United States, the territories of the US Virgin Islands and has touched many lives throughout Canada, Australia, the United Kingdom and the Eastern Caribbean by way of the several Radio Broadcast Networks she served. She launched the Prayer Breakers, a mentorship program in St. Croix, USVI in the summer of 2017 which she uses to sponsor training events annually.

Lady E. Nicholas is a servant leader at heart. She loves the people of God, and has a heart to see people prosper in every area of their lives. She carries a sense of refreshment everywhere she goes. It is evident in the relationships she forges and the friendships she fosters into unbreakable bonds. She is a people person, a pioneer in mobilizing Intercessors, Prayer Warriors, and Prophetic Watchmen. A Trailblazer in the 21st century Prayer Movement, leading the way in Virtual Prayer Conferences & online Prayer Revivals.

She is the Mother of three: Darion (Nick), Jahimba (Jay), and Amira (Myrah). One adopted spiritual son Mike J. Jr., one Daughter-in-Love, Lana J. and Grandmother of four: Mylik, Mykai, Taylor and Imani Joi. She is a resident of Laurel, Maryland.

Printed in the United States
By Bookmasters